Andrew Brodie Basics

LET'S DO MULTIPLICATION AND DIVISION

FOR AGES 5-6

with over **100** reward stickers

T0351847

- Over 400 practice questions
- Regular progress tests
- Matched to the National Curriculum

Published 2016 by Bloomsbury Publishing Plc
50 Bedford Square, London, WC1B 3DP

www.bloomsbury.com

Bloomsbury is a registered trademark of Bloomsbury Publishing Plc

ISBN 978-14729-2616-6

10 9 8 7 6 5 4 3 2 1

Printed in China by Leo Paper Products

This book is produced using paper that is made from wood grown in managed, sustainable forests. It is natural, renewable and recyclable. The logging and manufacturing processes conform to the environmental regulations of the country of origin.

To see our full range of titles visit www.bloomsbury.com

BLOOMSBURY

Introduction

This is the first in the series of *Andrew Brodie Basics: Let's Do Multiplication and Division* books. Each book contains more than 400 maths questions, deliberately designed to cover the following key aspects of the 'Number' section of the National Curriculum:

- Number and place value
- Multiplication and division.

Your child will get the most out of this series if you make time to discuss number knowledge as well as basic multiplication and division questions with them. Talk about real life situations such as sorting socks into pairs: How many socks are there? How many pairs of socks are there? In this way your child will begin to learn essential facts for the two times table, but will also start to understand the process of division: if there are three pairs of socks, there must be six socks – and if there are six socks, they can be sorted into three pairs. Mathematically, these processes can be shown as $3 \times 2 = 6$ and $6 \div 2 = 3$.

Children are not required to know notation for multiplication or division in Year 1. However, it is important that they learn to understand and use mathematical sentences, appreciating the meanings of the multiplication, division and equals signs, $x \div =$, and relating these to the vocabulary that they have learnt.

The level of difficulty is increased gradually throughout the book, but note that some questions are repeated. This is to ensure that children learn vital new facts: they may not know the answer to a particular question the first time they encounter it, but this provides the opportunity for you to help them to learn it for the next time that they come across it. Don't be surprised if they need to practise certain questions many times.

You may find that your child is challenged by some questions. Make sure that they don't lose confidence. Instead, encourage them to learn from their mistakes.

In Year 1, children are introduced to a wide range of new mathematical vocabulary. In relation to multiplication, children need to learn the use of expressions such as 'pairs', 'sets of', 'groups of', 'times' and 'double'. For division, they learn 'sorted into', 'shared between' and 'half'. The activities in this book provide opportunities for practising the use of this mathematical language.

Children gain confidence by learning facts that they can use in their future work. With lots of practice they will see their score improve and will learn to find maths both satisfying and enjoyable.

Look out for...

Maurice the Mouse, who provides useful tips and helpful advice throughout.

Brodie's Fast Five, quick-fire questions designed to test your child's mental arithmetic.

Odd and even numbers

Do you know which numbers are odd and which numbers are even?

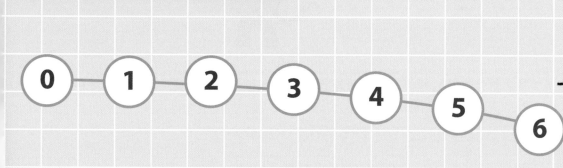

Colour the odd numbers red.
Colour the even numbers blue.

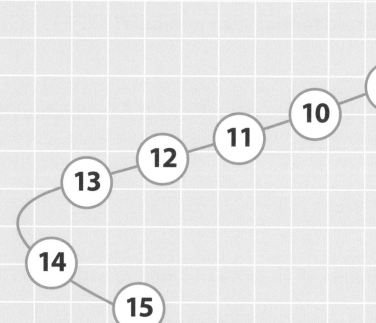

0 1 2 3 4 5 6 7 8 9 10 11 12 13 14 15 16 17 18 19 20

Brodie's Fast Five

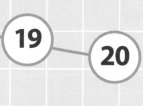

$2 + 2 =$ ⬜ $2 + 2 + 2 =$ ⬜

$2 + 2 + 2 + 2 =$ ⬜ $1 + 1 =$ ⬜ $3 + 3 =$ ⬜

Counting in twos

Can you count in twos, starting at any number?

1—2—3—4—5—6—7—8—9—10—11—12—13—14—15—16—17—18—19—20—21—22—23—24

1   **What shape has been used for the odd numbers?**

2   **What shape has been used for the even numbers?**

Look at the odd numbers below, then write the next two numbers in each set.

3   1 3 5 7

4   13 15 17 19

Look at the odd numbers below, then write the next two numbers in each set.

5   2 4 6 8

6   12 14 16 18

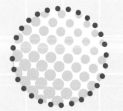

Brodie's Fast Five

2 + 2 + 2 =   2 + 2 + 2 + 2 =

2 + 2 + 2 + 2 + 2 =   4 + 4 =   5 + 5 =

Things in pairs

Lots of things come in sets of two, called 'pairs'.

Look at these sets.

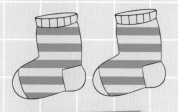
a pair of socks

a pair of gloves

a pair of eyes

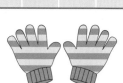  

1 How many gloves are there?

2 How many pairs of gloves are there?

3 How many socks are there?

4 How many pairs of socks are there?

5 How many eyes are there?

6 How many pairs of eyes are there?

Brodie's Fast Five

$2 + 2 =$

$2+2+2+2 =$

$2+2+2+2+2+2 =$

$3 + 3 =$

$5 + 5 =$

More pairs

Count the objects and the pairs.

Look at these sets.

1   How many gloves are there?

2   How many pairs of gloves are there?

3   How many socks are there?

4   How many pairs of socks are there?

5   How many eyes are there?

6   How many pairs of eyes are there?

7   How many wheels are there?

8   How many pairs of wheels are there?

Brodie's Fast Five

$2 + 2 + 2 =$ $10 + 10 =$

$2 + 2 + 2 + 2 + 2 =$ $3 + 3 =$ $5 + 5 =$

Even more pairs!

Keep counting the objects and the pairs!

Look at these sets.

1 How many gloves are there?

2 How many pairs of gloves are there?

3 How many socks are there?

4 How many pairs of socks are there?

5 How many eyes are there?

6 How many pairs of eyes are there?

7 How many wheels are there?

8 How many pairs of wheels are there?

Brodie's Fast Five

$2 + 2 + 2 =$ $2 + 2 + 2 + 2 =$

$2+2+2+2+2+2+2 =$ $6 + 6 =$ $7 + 7 =$

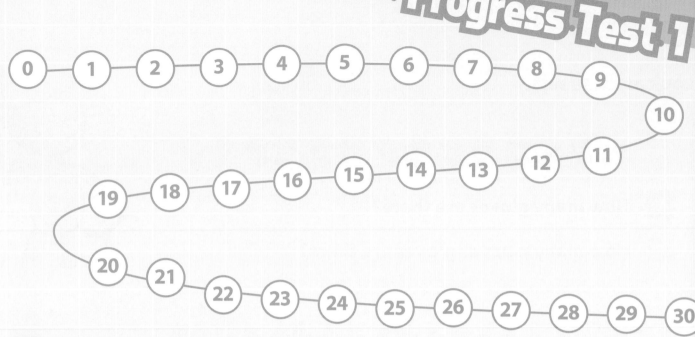

1 Colour the odd numbers red.

2 Colour the even numbers blue.

3 Draw 6 pairs of socks.

4 How many socks did you draw?

5 How many gloves are there?

6 How many pairs of gloves are there?

7 How many wheels are there?

8 How many pairs of wheels are there?

Counting in fives

You have five fingers on each hand. You can use them to help with your counting!

Look at the number of fingers in each picture.

5 fingers

10 fingers

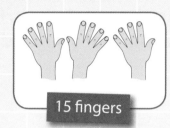
15 fingers

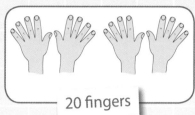
20 fingers

1 **Write down how many fingers are in each picture.**

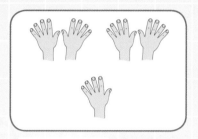
_____ **fingers**

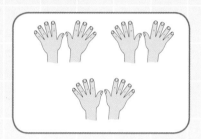
_____ **fingers**

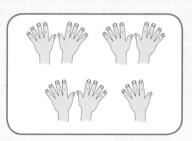
_____ **fingers**

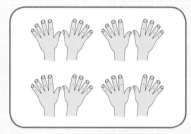
_____ **fingers**

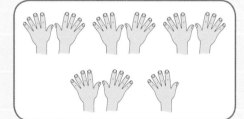
_____ **fingers**

_____ **fingers**

2 **Write the numbers out again. The first two have been done for you.**

5   10

Brodie's Fast Five

5 + 5 =

5 + 5 + 5 =

5 + 5 + 5 + 5 =

2 + 2 + 2 =

4 + 4 =

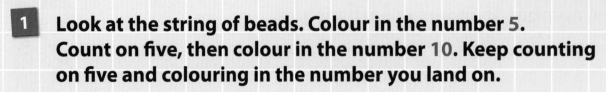

More counting in fives

Can you count in fives?

1 Look at the string of beads. Colour in the number 5. Count on five, then colour in the number 10. Keep counting on five and colouring in the number you land on.

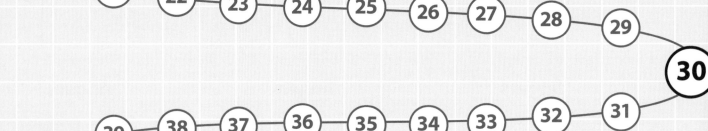

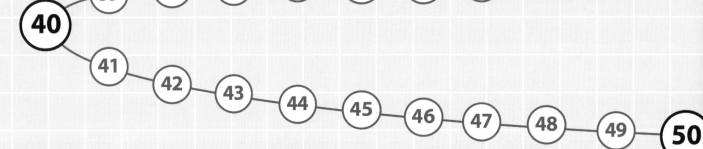

2 Which numbers did you colour in?

Brodie's Fast Five

5 + 5 =

5 + 5 + 5 + 5 =

10 + 10 =

2 + 2 + 2 + 2 =

4 + 4 =

Counting dots on dice 1

There are 6 different numbers of dots on a dice.

1 How many dice are there?

2 How many dots are there altogether?

3 How many dice are there?

4 How many dots are there altogether?

5 How many dice are there?

6 How many dots are there altogether?

7 How many dice are there?

8 How many dots are there altogether?

Brodie's Fast Five

$5 + 5 + 5 =$

$5 + 5 + 5 + 5 =$

$5 + 5 + 5 + 5 + 5 =$

$5 + 5 + 2 + 2 =$

$3 + 3 =$

Counting dots on dice 2

1 How many dice are there?

2 How many dots are there altogether?

3 How many dice are there?

4 How many dots are there altogether?

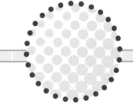

5 How many dice are there?

6 How many dots are there altogether?

7 How many dice are there?

8 How many dots are there altogether?

9 How many dice are there?

10 How many dots are there altogether?

Brodie's Fast Five

$5 + 5 + 5 =$

$5 + 5 + 5 + 5 + 5 =$

$5 + 5 + 5 + 5 + 5 + 5 =$

$2 + 2 + 2 + 2 =$

$4 + 4 =$

Fives on a hundred square

Can you count to a hundred?

1 Look at the square below. Colour in the number 5.
Count on five, then colour in the number 10.
Keep counting on five and colouring in the
number you land on.

1	2	3	4	5	6	7	8	9	10
11	12	13	14	15	16	17	18	19	20
21	22	23	24	25	26	27	28	29	30
31	32	33	34	35	36	37	38	39	40
41	42	43	44	45	46	47	48	49	50
51	52	53	54	55	56	57	58	59	60
61	62	63	64	65	66	67	68	69	70
71	72	73	74	75	76	77	78	79	80
81	82	83	84	85	86	87	88	89	90
91	92	93	94	95	96	97	98	99	100

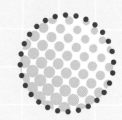

2 Which numbers did you colour in?

Brodie's Fast Five

$5 + 5 + 5 + 5 =$ $\qquad$ $5 + 5 + 5 =$

$5 + 5 + 5 + 5 + 5 =$ $\qquad$ $2 + 2 + 2 + 2 + 2 =$ $\qquad$ $5 + 5 + 5 + 2 + 2 =$

Count how many fingers are being held up in each picture.

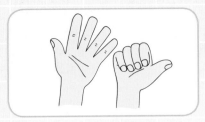 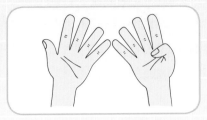

1 [_____] fingers   **2** [_____] fingers

3 Look at the string of beads. Colour in the number **25**. Count on five, then colour in the number **30**. Keep counting on five and colouring in the number you land on.

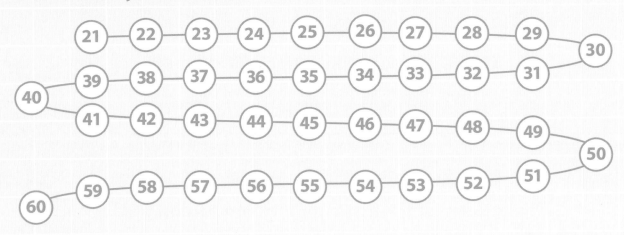

Which numbers did you colour in?

4 How many dice are there?

5 How many dots are there altogether?

6 How many dice are there?

7 How many dots are there altogether?

Tens on a hundred square

How quickly can you count to a hundred?

1 Look at the number square below. Colour in the number 10. Count on ten, then colour in the number 20. Keep counting on ten and colouring in the number you land on.

1	2	3	4	5	6	7	8	9	10
11	12	13	14	15	16	17	18	19	20
21	22	23	24	25	26	27	28	29	30
31	32	33	34	35	36	37	38	39	40
41	42	43	44	45	46	47	48	49	50
51	52	53	54	55	56	57	58	59	60
61	62	63	64	65	66	67	68	69	70
71	72	73	74	75	76	77	78	79	80
81	82	83	84	85	86	87	88	89	90
91	92	93	94	95	96	97	98	99	100

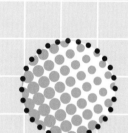

2 Which numbers did you colour?

3 Now colour in the number 2 on the number square. Count on two, then colour in the number 4. Keep counting on two and colouring, all the way to 100. You have coloured the tens already!

Brodie's Fast Five

10 + 10 =   10 + 10 + 10 =

10 + 10 + 10 + 10 =   2 + 2 + 2 + 2 =   5 + 5 + 5 =

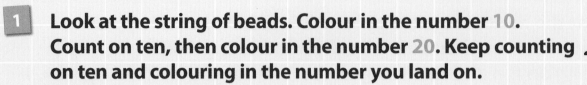

Counting in tens

1 Look at the string of beads. Colour in the number 10.
Count on ten, then colour in the number 20. Keep counting
on ten and colouring in the number you land on.

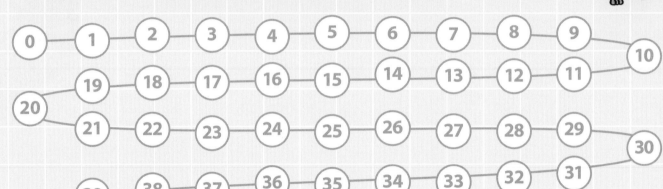

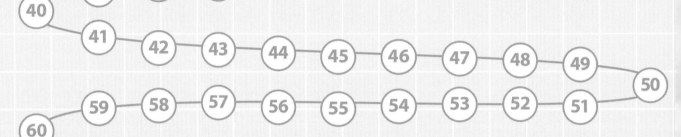

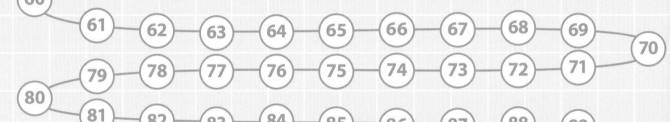

2 Which numbers did you colour?

Brodie's Fast Five

10 + 10 =   10 + 10 + 10 + 10 =

10+10+10+10+10 =   2+2+2+2+2 =   5+5+5+5 =

The ten times table

Can you count in tens to one hundred?

Ten fingers altogether.
One set of ten is ten altogether.
We say one ten is ten.
We write this number sentence as 1 x 10 = 10

Two tens are twenty. 2 x 10 = 20

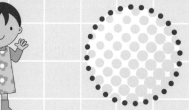

---

1 **How many fingers do the children have altogether?** 3 x 10 =

---

2 **How many fingers do the children have altogether?** 4 x 10 =

---

3 **How many fingers do the children have altogether?** 5 x 10 =

Brodie's Fast Five

10 + 10 + 10 =   10 + 10 + 10 + 10 =

10 + 10 + 10 + 10 + 10 =   10 + 2 + 2 =   10 + 5 + 5 =

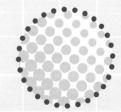

On the last page you started to write out the ten times table.

Multiplication

Here is the ten times table. Can you fill in the missing numbers? The first one has been done for you.

1	One ten is ten.		$1 \times 10 = 10$
2	Two tens are twenty.		$2 \times 10 =$
3	Three threes are nine.		$3 \times 10 =$
4	Four tens are forty.		$4 \times 10 =$
5	Five tens are fifty.		$5 \times 10 =$
6	Six tens are sixty.		$6 \times 10 =$
7	Seven tens are seventy.		$7 \times 10 =$
8	Eight tens are eighty.		$8 \times 10 =$
9	Nine tens are ninety.		$9 \times 10 =$
10	Ten tens are a hundred.		$10 \times 10 =$
11	Eleven tens are a hundred and ten.		$11 \times 10 =$
12	Twelve tens are a hundred and twenty.		$12 \times 10 =$

Division

13 How many sets of ten make twenty altogether?

14 How many tens make thirty?

15 How many tens make forty?

16 How many tens make fifty?

17 How many tens make sixty?

18 How many tens make seventy?

19 How many tens make eighty?

20 How many tens make ninety?

21 How many tens make a hundred?

22 How many tens make a hundred and ten?

23 How many tens make a hundred and twenty?

Money

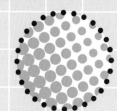

Ten ten pence coins are worth a whole pound!

 $1 \times 10p = 10p$

 $2 \times 10p = 20p$

 $3 \times 10p = 30p$

  $4 \times 10p = 40p$

    $5 \times 10p = 50p$

1 How many 10p coins are worth 40p?

2 Three children share 30p. How much does each child have?

3 If I share 50p between five people, how much would they each have?

Brodie's Fast Five

$10 + 10 = $ $2 \times 10 = $

$10 + 10 + 10 + 10 = $ $4 \times 10 = $ $5 + 5 + 5 = $

Multiplication

1 5 x 10 =

2 8 x 10 =

3 2 x 10 =

4 9 x 10 =

5 6 x 10 =

6 4 x 10 =

7 7 x 10 =

8 3 x 10 =

9 10 x 10 =

10 11 x 10 =

Division

11 How many tens make seventy?

12 How many tens make thirty?

13 How many tens make ninety?

14 How many tens make twenty?

15 How many tens make eighty?

16 How many tens make forty?

17 How many tens make a hundred?

18 How many tens make fifty?

19 How many tens make sixty?

20 Four children share 40p. How much money does each child have?

I like ladybirds. Some ladybirds only have two spots!

Look at this picture.

1 How many ladybirds are there?

2 How many spots are there?

One set of two is two altogether.

We say **one two is two**. We write $1 \times 2 = 2$

Two twos are four. $2 \times 2 = 4$

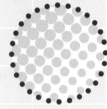

---

3 How many spots do these ladybirds have altogether? $3 \times 2 =$

---

4 How many spots do these ladybirds have altogether? $4 \times 2 =$

---

5 How many spots do these ladybirds have altogether? $5 \times 2 =$

Brodie's Fast Five

$3 \times 10 =$ $\qquad$ $4 \times 10 =$

$5 \times 10 =$ $\qquad$ $3 \times 2 =$ $\qquad$ $5 \times 2 =$

Keep counting ladybirds and their spots!

1 How many spots do these ladybirds have altogether? 6 x 2 =

2 How many spots do these ladybirds have altogether? 7 x 2 =

3 How many spots do these ladybirds have altogether? 8 x 2 =

4 How many spots do these ladybirds have altogether? 9 x 2 =

5 How many spots do these ladybirds have altogether? 10 x 2 =

6 How many spots do these ladybirds have altogether? 11 x 2 =

7 How many spots do these ladybirds have altogether? 12 x 2 =

Brodie's Fast Five

10 + 10 + 10 =   3 x 10 =

10 + 10 + 10 + 10 + 10 + 10 =   6 x 10 =   2 x 2 =

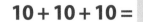

The two times table

Multiplication

Here is the two times table. Can you fill in the missing numbers?
The first one has been done for you.

1	One two is two.	➡	1 x 2 = 2
2	Two twos are four.	➡	2 x 2 =
3	Three twos are six.	➡	3 x 2 =
4	Four twos are eight.	➡	4 x 2 =
5	Five twos are ten.	➡	5 x 2 =
6	Six twos are twelve.	➡	6 x 2 =
7	Seven twos are fourteen.	➡	7 x 2 =
8	Eight twos are sixteen.	➡	8 x 2 =
9	Nine twos are eighteen.	➡	9 x 2 =
10	Ten twos are twenty.	➡	10 x 2 =
11	Eleven twos are twenty-two.	➡	11 x 2 =
12	Twelve twos are twenty-four.	➡	12 x 2 =

Division

13 How many sets of two make four altogether?

14 How many twos make six?

15 How many twos make eight?

16 How many twos make ten?

17 How many twos make twelve?

18 How many twos make fourteen?

19 How many twos make sixteen?

20 How many twos make eighteen?

21 How many twos make twenty?

22 How many twos make twenty-two?

23 How many twos make twenty-four?

On the last pages you started to write out the two times table.

Money multiplication

Ten two pence coins are worth twenty pence!

Fill in the missing numbers. Some have been done for you.

1 1 x 2p = **2p**

2 2 x 2p = **4p**

3 3 x 2p = **6p**

4 4x 2p =

5 5 x 2p =

6 6 x 2p =

7 7 x 2p =

8 8 x 2p =

9 9 x 2p =

10 10 x 2p =

11 11 x 2p =

12 12 x 2p =

Brodie's Fast Five

8 x 10 =   3 x 10 =

9 x 10 =   10 x 10 =   5 x 2 =

Money division

You could use page 24 to help with your answers to these questions!

1. How many 2p coins are worth 12p?

2. How many 2p coins are worth 4p?

3. How many 2p coins are worth 10p?

4. How many 2p coins are worth 18p?

5. How many 2p coins are worth 8p?

6. How many 2p coins are worth 14p?

7. How many 2p coins are worth 22p?

8. How many 2p coins are worth 6p?

9. How many 2p coins are worth 16p?

10. How many 2p coins are worth 20p?

11. How many 2p coins are worth 24p?

Brodie's Fast Five

10 + 10 + 10 + 10 =   4 x 10 =

10 + 10 + 10 + 10 + 10 =   5 x 10 =   8 x 2 =

1 How many gloves altogether? 6 x 2 =

2 How many socks altogether? 7 x 2 =

3 How many spots altogether? 8 x 2 =

4 How many hands altogether? 9 x 2 =

5 How many sets of two make four altogether?

6 How many twos make six?

7 How many twos make eight?

8 How many twos make ten?

9 How many 2p coins are worth 12p?

10 How many 2p coins are worth 14p?

11 How many 2p coins are worth 16p?

12 How many 2p coins are worth 18p?

Making the five times table 1

Have you ever seen a starfish in real life?

Here is 1 starfish.

A starfish has 5 arms.

One set of five is five altogether.

We say one five is five. We write $1 \times 5 = 5$

Two fives are ten. $2 \times 5 = 10$

1 **How many arms do these starfish have altogether?** $3 \times 5 =$

2 **How many arms do these starfish have altogether?** $4 \times 5 =$

3 **How many arms do these starfish have altogether?** $5 \times 5 =$

Brodie's Fast Five

$5 + 5 + 5 =$ $3 \times 5 =$

$5 + 5 + 5 + 5 + 5 + 5 =$ $6 \times 5 =$ $2 \times 5 =$

27

Keep counting starfish and their arms!

1 How many arms do these starfish have altogether? 6 x 5 =

2 How many arms do these starfish have altogether? 7 x 5 =

3 How many arms do these starfish have altogether? 8 x 5 =

4 How many arms do these starfish have altogether? 9 x 5 =

5 How many arms do these starfish have altogether? 10 x 5 =

6 How many arms do these starfish have altogether? 11 x 5 =

7 How many arms do these starfish have altogether? 12 x 5 =

Brodie's Fast Five

6 x 10 =   9 x 10 =

5 + 5 + 5 + 5 + 5 + 5 =   6 x 5 =   12 x 5 =

The five times table

Do you know your five times table?

Multiplication

Here is the five times table. Can you fill in the missing numbers?
One has been done for you.

1	One five is five.	⟶	1 x 5 = 5
2	Two fives are ten.	⟶	2 x 5 =
3	Three fives are fifteen.	⟶	3 x 5 =
4	Four fives are twenty.	⟶	4 x 5 =
5	Five fives are twenty-five.	⟶	5 x 5 =
6	Six fives are thirty.	⟶	6 x 5 =
7	Seven fives are thirty-five.	⟶	7 x 5 =
8	Eight fives are forty.	⟶	8 x 5 =
9	Nine fives are forty-five.	⟶	9 x 5 =
10	Ten fives are fifty.	⟶	10 x 5 =
11	Eleven fives are fifty-five.	⟶	11 x 5 =
12	Twelve fives are sixty.	⟶	12 x 5 =

Division

13 How many sets of five make ten altogether?

14 How many fives make fifteen?

15 How many fives make twenty?

16 How many fives make twenty-five?

17 How many fives make thirty?

18 How many fives make thirty-five?

19 How many fives make forty?

20 How many fives make forty-five?

21 How many fives make fifty?

22 How many fives make fifty-five?

23 How many fives make sixty?

Money multiplication

Ten five pence coins are worth fifty pence.

Fill in the missing numbers. Some have been done for you.

1   1 x 5p =   *5p*

2   2 x 5p =   *10p*

3   3 x 5p =   *15p*

4   4 x 5p =

5   5 x 5p =

6   6 x 5p =

7   7 x 5p =

8   8 x 5p =

9   9 x 5p =

10   10 x 5p =

11   11 x 5p =

12   12 x 5p =

Brodie's Fast Five

7 x 10 =   3 x 5 =

2 x 10 =   6 x 2 =   5 x 5 =

Money division

You could use page 30 to help with your answers to these questions!

1 How many 5p coins are worth 10p?

2 How many 5p coins are worth 15p?

3 How many 5p coins are worth 20p?

4 How many 5p coins are worth 25p?

5 How many 5p coins are worth 30p?

6 How many 5p coins are worth 35p?

7 How many 5p coins are worth 40p?

8 How many 5p coins are worth 45p?

9 How many 5p coins are worth 50p?

10 How many 5p coins are worth 55p?

11 How many 5p coins are worth 60p?

Brodie's Fast Five

12 x 10 =   **5 x 10 =**

9 x 2 =   **8 x 5 =**   **7 x 2 =**

31

1 How many arms do the starfish have altogether? 6 x 5 =

2 How many fingers do the hands have altogether? 7 x 5 =

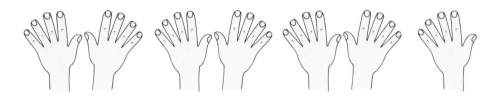

3 How many dots can you see altogether? 9 x 5 =

4 How many sets of five make ten altogether?

5 How many fives make fifteen?

6 How many fives make twenty?

7 How many fives make twenty-five?

8 How many 5p coins are worth 10p?

9 How many 5p coins are worth 15p?

10 How many 5p coins are worth 20p?

11 How many 5p coins are worth 25p?

Arrays can help with multiplication.

This array of squares shows one set of two.

 This is the number sentence: 1 x 2 = 2

This array of squares shows two sets of two.

 2 x 2 = 4

This array of squares shows three sets of two.

3 x 2 = 6

Write the multiplication sentences for each of the arrays below.

1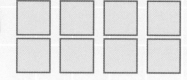

3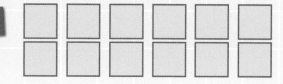

2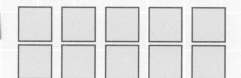

4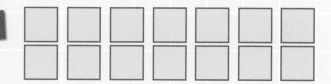

Brodie's Fast Five

8 x 10 =   7 x 5 =

10 x 2 =   6 x 5 =   2 x 10 =

Here are some more arrays showing the two times table.

Write the multiplication sentences for each of the arrays below.

1

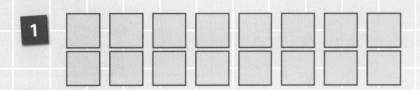

2

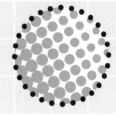

3

4

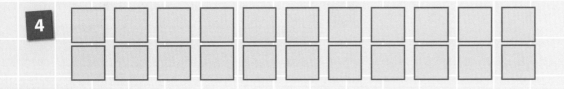

5

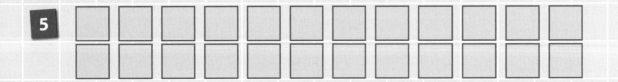

6   **Write the two times table in the boxes below. It has been started for you.**

1 x 2 = 2	2 x 2 = 4			

Write the multiplication sentences for each of the arrays below.

 **This is the number sentence:** 1 x 5 = 5

Arrays can help with multiplication.

This array of squares shows two sets of five.

 2 x 5 = 10

This array of squares shows three sets of five.

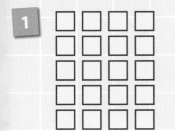 3 x 5 = 15

Write the multiplication sentences for each of the arrays below.

1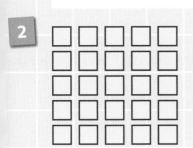

3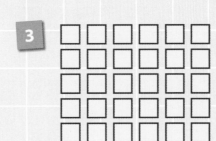

2

4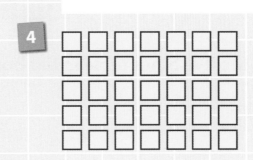

Here are some more arrays showing the five times table.

Write the multiplication sentences for each of the arrays below.

1
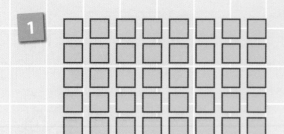

2
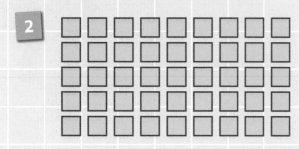

3
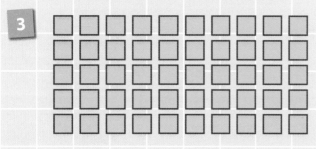

4
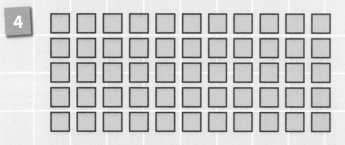

5

6 **Write the five times table in the boxes below. It has been started for you.**

1 x 5 = 5	2 x 5 = 10			

36

Arrays with objects

I can't see any mice in these arrays!

Write the multiplication number sentence for each array.

1

2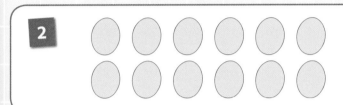

3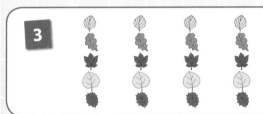

4

5

6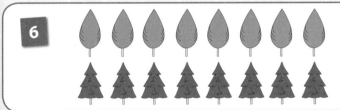

Brodie's Fast Five

5 x 5 =   9 x 5 =

3 x 5 =   11 x 5 =   12 x 5 =

1 How quickly can you write the two times table?
It has been started for you.

$1 \times 2 = 2$ $2 \times 2 = 4$

2 How quickly can you write the five times table?
It has been started for you.

$1 \times 5 = 5$ $2 \times 5 = 10$

There is a special way of writing division sentences.

Here is the two times table again.
Can you fill in the missing numbers?

#			
1	One two is two.	→	1 x 2 = 2
2	Two twos are four.	→	2 x 2 =
3	Three twos are six.	→	3 x 2 =
4	Four twos are eight.	→	4 x 2 =
5	Five twos are ten.	→	5 x 2 =
6	Six twos are twelve.	→	6 x 2 =
7	Seven twos are fourteen.	→	7 x 2 =
8	Eight twos are sixteen.	→	8 x 2 =
9	Nine twos are eighteen.	→	9 x 2 =
10	Ten twos are twenty.	→	10 x 2 =
11	Eleven twos are twenty-two.	→	11 x 2 =
12	Twelve twos are twenty-four.	→	12 x 2 =

Look at the questions and division sentences below. Write your answers in the boxes. The first two have been done for you.

13 How many sets of two make four altogether? $4 \div 2 = 2$

14 How many twos make six? $6 \div 2 = 3$

15 How many twos make eight? $8 \div 2 =$

16 How many twos make ten? $10 \div 2 =$

17 How many twos make twelve? $12 \div 2 =$

18 How many twos make fourteen? $14 \div 2 =$

19 How many twos make sixteen? $16 \div 2 =$

20 How many twos make eighteen? $18 \div 2 =$

21 How many twos make twenty? $20 \div 2 =$

22 How many twos make twenty-two? $22 \div 2 =$

23 How many twos make twenty-four? $24 \div 2 =$

**Here is the five times table again.
Can you fill in the missing numbers?**

1	One five is five.	$\longrightarrow$	1 x 5 = 5
2	Two fives are ten.	$\longrightarrow$	2 x 5 =
3	Three fives are fifteen.	$\longrightarrow$	3 x 5 =
4	Four fives are twenty.	$\longrightarrow$	4 x 5 =
5	Five fives are twenty-five.	$\longrightarrow$	5 x 5 =
6	Six fives are thirty.	$\longrightarrow$	6 x 5 =
7	Seven fives are thirty-five.	$\longrightarrow$	7 x 5 =
8	Eight fives are forty.	$\longrightarrow$	8 x 5 =
9	Nine fives are forty-five.	$\longrightarrow$	9 x 5 =
10	Ten fives are fifty.	$\longrightarrow$	10 x 5 =
11	Eleven fives are fifty-five.	$\longrightarrow$	11 x 5 =
12	Twelve fives are sixty.	$\longrightarrow$	12 x 5 =

Look at the questions and division sentences below. Write your answers in the boxes. The first two have been done for you.

13	How many sets of five make ten altogether?	$10 \div 5 = 2$
14	How many fives make fifteen?	$15 \div 5 = 3$
15	How many fives make twenty?	$20 \div 5 =$
16	How many fives make twenty-five?	$25 \div 5 =$
17	How many fives make thirty?	$30 \div 5 =$
18	How many fives make thirty-five?	$35 \div 5 =$
19	How many fives make forty?	$40 \div 5 =$
20	How many fives make forty-five?	$45 \div 5 =$
21	How many fives make fifty?	$50 \div 5 =$
22	How many fives make fifty-five?	$55 \div 5 =$
23	How many fives make sixty?	$60 \div 5 =$

Do you remember how to write division sentences?

Here is the ten times table again.
Can you fill in the missing numbers?

1	One ten is ten.	→	1 x 10 = *10*
2	Two tens are twenty.	→	2 x 10 =
3	Three tens are thirty.	→	3 x 10 =
4	Four tens are forty.	→	4 x 10 =
5	Five tens are fifty.	→	5 x 10 =
6	Six tens are sixty.	→	6 x 10 =
7	Seven tens are seventy.	→	7 x 10 =
8	Eight tens are eighty.	→	8 x 10 =
9	Nine tens are ninety.	→	9 x 10 =
10	Ten tens are a hundred.	→	10 x 10 =
11	Eleven tens are a hundred and ten.	→	11 x 10 =
12	Twelve tens are a hundred and twenty.	→	12 x 10 =

Look at the questions and division sentences below. Write your answers in the boxes. The first two have been done for you.

13   How many sets of ten make twenty altogether? $20 \div 10 = 2$

14   How many tens make thirty? $30 \div 10 = 3$

15   How many tens make forty? $40 \div 10 =$

16   How many tens make fifty? $50 \div 10 =$

17   How many tens make sixty? $60 \div 10 =$

18   How many tens make seventy? $70 \div 10 =$

19   How many tens make eighty? $80 \div 10 =$

20   How many tens make ninety? $90 \div 10 =$

21   How many tens make a hundred? $100 \div 10 =$

22   How many tens make a hundred and ten? $110 \div 10 =$

23   How many tens make a hundred and twenty? $120 \div 10 =$

Money division with 2p coins

Eight 2p coins are worth 16p.

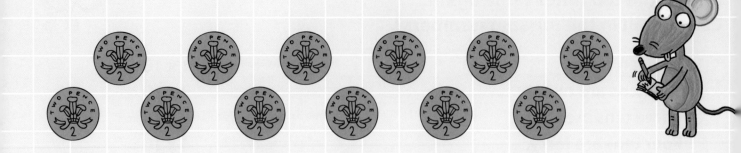

1 How many 2p coins are worth 12p?

2 How many 2p coins are worth 4p?

3 How many 2p coins are worth 10p?

4 How many 2p coins are worth 18p?

5 How many 2p coins are worth 8p?

6 How many 2p coins are worth 14p?

7 How many 2p coins are worth 22p?

8 How many 2p coins are worth 6p?

9 How many 2p coins are worth 16p?

10 How many 2p coins are worth 20p?

11 How many 2p coins are worth 24p?

Brodie's Fast Five

3 x 10 =   8 x 10 =

12 x 10 =   6 x 10 =   10 x 10 =

Money division with 5p coins

Ten 5p coins are worth 50p.

1	How many 5p coins are worth 60p?	
2	How many 5p coins are worth 20p?	
3	How many 5p coins are worth 45p?	
4	How many 5p coins are worth 10p?	
5	How many 5p coins are worth 50p?	
6	How many 5p coins are worth 30p?	
7	How many 5p coins are worth 15p?	
8	How many 5p coins are worth 40p?	
9	How many 5p coins are worth 55p?	
10	How many 5p coins are worth 35p?	
11	How many 5p coins are worth 25p?	

Brodie's Fast Five

$3 \times 2 =$ $8 \times 2 =$

$12 \times 2 =$ $6 \times 2 =$ $10 \times 2 =$

1 Write out the two times table, the five times table and the ten times table as fast as you can.

2 times table	5 times table	10 times table

2 How many 2p coins are worth 18p?

3 How many 2p coins are worth 6p?

4 How many 2p coins are worth 14p?

5 How many 5p coins are worth 40p?

6 How many 5p coins are worth 15p?

7 How many 5p coins are worth 55p?

ANSWERS

Page 3 • Odd and even numbers

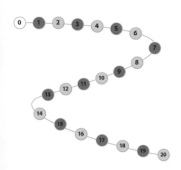

Brodie's Fast Five
1. 4
2. 6
3. 8
4. 2
5. 6

Page 4 • Counting in twos

1. Circle
2. Square
3. 9   11
4. 21   23
5. 10   12
6. 20   22

Brodie's Fast Five
1. 6
2. 8
3. 10
4. 8
5. 10

Page 5 • Things in pairs

1. 6
2. 3
3. 4
4. 2
5. 8
6. 4

Brodie's Fast Five
1. 4
2. 8
3. 12
4. 6
5. 10

Page 6 • More pairs

1. 2
2. 1
3. 10
4. 5
5. 12
6. 6
7. 8
8. 4

Brodie's Fast Five
1. 6
2. 20
3. 10
4. 6
5. 10

Page 7 • Even more pairs!

1. 14
2. 7
3. 20
4. 10
5. 16
6. 8
7. 18
8. 9

Brodie's Fast Five
1. 6
2. 8
3. 14
4. 12
5. 14

Page 8 • Progress Test 1

1. and 2.

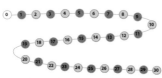

3. Check that your child has drawn 6 pairs of socks
4. 12
5. 16
6. 8
7. 20
8. 10

Page 9 • Counting in fives

1. 25 30 35 40 45 50
2. 5 10 15 20 25 30 35 40 45 50

Brodie's Fast Five
1. 10
2. 15
3. 20
4. 6
5. 8

Page 10 • More counting in fives

1.

2. 5 10 15 20 25 30 35 40 45 50

Brodie's Fast Five
1. 10
2. 20
3. 20
4. 8
5. 8

Page 11 • Counting dots on dice 1

1. 2
2. 10
3. 3
4. 15
5. 4
6. 20
7. 5
8. 25

Brodie's Fast Five
1. 15
2. 20
3. 25
4. 14
5. 6

Page 12 • Counting dots on dice 2

1. 6
2. 30
3. 7
4. 35
5. 8
6. 40
7. 9
8. 45
9. 10
10. 50

Brodie's Fast Five
1. 15
2. 25
3. 30
4. 8
5. 8

Page 13 • Fives on a hundred square

1.

1	2	3	4	5	6	7	8	9	10
11	12	13	14	15	16	17	18	19	20
21	22	23	24	25	26	27	28	29	30
31	32	33	34	35	36	37	38	39	40
41	42	43	44	45	46	47	48	49	50
51	52	53	54	55	56	57	58	59	60
61	62	63	64	65	66	67	68	69	70
71	72	73	74	75	76	77	78	79	80
81	82	83	84	85	86	87	88	89	90
91	92	93	94	95	96	97	98	99	100

2. 5 10 15 20 25 30 35 40 45 50 55 60 65 70 75 80 85 90 95 100

Brodie's Fast Five
1. 10
2. 20
3. 20
4. 8
5. 8

Page 14 • Progress Test 2

1. 6 fingers
2. 9 fingers
3.

21	22	23	24	**25**	26	27	28	29	**30**
40	39	38	37	36	**35**	34	33	32	31
41	42	43	44	**45**	46	47	48	49	**50**
60	59	58	57	56	**55**	54	53	52	51

4. 25 30 35 40 45 50 55 60
5. 3
6. 15
7. 6
8. 30

Page 15 • Tens on a hundred square

1.

1	2	3	4	5	6	7	8	9	10
11	12	13	14	15	16	17	18	19	20
21	22	23	24	25	26	27	28	29	30
31	32	33	34	35	36	37	38	39	40
41	42	43	44	45	46	47	48	49	50
51	52	53	54	55	56	57	58	59	60
61	62	63	64	65	66	67	68	69	70
71	72	73	74	75	76	77	78	79	80
81	82	83	84	85	86	87	88	89	90
91	92	93	94	95	96	97	98	99	100

2. 10 20 30 40 50 60 70 80 90 100

3.

1	2	3	4	5	6	7	8	9	10
11	12	13	14	15	16	17	18	19	20
21	22	23	24	25	26	27	28	29	30
31	32	33	34	35	36	37	38	39	40
41	42	43	44	45	46	47	48	49	50
51	52	53	54	55	56	57	58	59	60
61	62	63	64	65	66	67	68	69	70
71	72	73	74	75	76	77	78	79	80
81	82	83	84	85	86	87	88	89	90
91	92	93	94	95	96	97	98	99	100

Brodie's Fast Five
1. 20
2. 30
3. 40
4. 8
5. 15

Page 16 • Counting in tens

1.

2. 10 20 30 40 50 60 70 80 90 100

1. 20
2. 40
3. 50
4. 10
5. 20

Page 17 • The ten times table

1. 30
2. 40
3. 50

Brodie's Fast Five

1. 30
2. 40
3. 50
4. 14
5. 20

Page 18 • More of the ten times table

Multiplication

1. 10
2. 20
3. 30
4. 40
5. 50
6. 60
7. 70
8. 80
9. 90
10. 100
11. 110
12. 120

Division

13. 2
14. 3
15. 4
16. 5
17. 6
18. 7
19. 8
20. 9
21. 10
22. 11
23. 12

Page 19 • Money

1. 4
2. 10p
3. 10p

Brodie's Fast Five

1. 20
2. 20
3. 40
4. 40
5. 15

Page 20 • Progress Test 3

Multiplication

1. 50
2. 80
3. 20
4. 90
5. 60
6. 40
7. 70
8. 30
9. 100
10. 110

Division

11. 7
12. 3
13. 9
14. 2
15. 8
16. 4
17. 10
18. 5
19. 6
20. 10p

Page 21 • Making the two times table 1

1. 1
2. 2
3. 6
4. 8
5. 10

Brodie's Fast Five

1. 30
2. 40
3. 50
4. 6
5. 10

Page 22 • Making the two times table 2

1. 12
2. 14
3. 16
4. 18
5. 20
6. 22
7. 24

Brodie's Fast Five

1. 30
2. 30
3. 60
4. 60
5. 4

Page 23 • The two times table

Multiplication

1. 2
2. 4
3. 6
4. 8
5. 10
6. 12
7. 14
8. 16
9. 18
10. 20
11. 22
12. 24

Division

13. 2
14. 3
15. 4
16. 5
17. 6
18. 7
19. 8
20. 9
21. 10
22. 11
23. 12

Page 24 • Money multiplication

1. 2p
2. 4p
3. 6p
4. 8p
5. 10p
6. 12p
7. 14p
8. 16p
9. 18p
10. 20p
11. 22p
12. 24p

Brodie's Fast Five

1. 80
2. 30
3. 90
4. 100
5. 10

Page 25 • Money division

1. 6
2. 2
3. 5
4. 9
5. 4
6. 7
7. 11
8. 3
9. 8
10. 10
11. 12

Brodie's Fast Five

1. 40
2. 40
3. 50
4. 50
5. 16

Page 26 • Progress Test 4

1. 12
2. 14
3. 16
4. 18
5. 2
6. 3
7. 4
8. 5
9. 6
10. 7
11. 8
12. 9

Page 27 • Making the five times table 1

1. 15
2. 20
3. 25

Brodie's Fast Five

1. 15
2. 15
3. 30
4. 30
5. 10

Page 28 • Making the five times table 2

1. 30
2. 35
3. 40
4. 45
5. 50
6. 55
7. 60

Brodie's Fast Five

1. 60
2. 90
3. 30
4. 30
5. 60

Page 29 • The five times table

Multiplication

1. 5
2. 10
3. 15
4. 20
5. 25
6. 30
7. 35
8. 40
9. 45
10. 50
11. 55
12. 60

Division

13. 2
14. 3
15. 4
16. 5
17. 6
18. 7
19. 8
20. 9
21. 10
22. 11
23. 12

Page 30 • Money multiplication

1. 5p
2. 10p
3. 15p
4. 20p
5. 25p
6. 30p
7. 35p
8. 40p
9. 45p
10. 50p
11. 55p
12. 60p

Brodie's Fast Five

1. 70
2. 15
3. 20
4. 12
5. 25

Page 31 • Money division

1. 2
2. 3
3. 4
4. 5
5. 6
6. 7
7. 8
8. 9
9. 10
10. 11
11. 12

Brodie's Fast Five

1. 120
2. 50
3. 18
4. 40
5. 14

Page 32 • Progress Test 5

1. 30
2. 35
3. 45
4. 2
5. 3
6. 4
7. 5
8. 2
9. 3
10. 4
11. 5

Page 33 • Arrays showing the two times table

1. 4 x 2 = 8
2. 5 x 2 = 10
3. 6 x 2 = 12
4. 7 x 2 = 14

Brodie's Fast Five

1. 80
2. 35
3. 20
4. 30
5. 20

Page 34 • Arrays to help with multiplication

1. 8 x 2 = 16
2. 9 x 2 = 18
3. 10 x 2 = 20
4. 11 x 2 = 22
5. 12 x 2 = 24
6. 1 x 2 = 2
   2 x 2 = 4
   3 x 2 = 6
   4 x 2 = 8
   5 x 2 = 10
   6 x 2 = 12
   7 x 2 = 14
   8 x 2 = 16
   9 x 2 = 18
   10 x 2 = 20
   11 x 2 = 22
   12 x 2 = 24

Page 35 • Arrays showing the five times table 1

1. 4 x 5 = 20
2. 5 x 5 = 25
3. 6 x 5 = 30
4. 7 x 5 = 35

Page 36 • Arrays showing the five times table 2

1. 8 x 5 = 40
2. 9 x 5 = 45
3. 10 x 5 = 50
4. 11 x 5 = 55
5. 12 x 5 = 60

6. 1 x 5 = 5
   2 x 5 = 10
   3 x 5 = 15
   4 x 5 = 20
   5 x 5 = 25
   6 x 5 = 30
   7 x 5 = 35
   8 x 5 = 40
   9 x 5 = 45
   10 x 5 = 50
   11 x 5 = 55
   12 x 5 = 60

Page 37 • Arrays with objects

1. 3 x 2 = 6
2. 6 x 2 = 12
3. 4 x 5 = 20
4. 7 x 2 = 14
5. 5 x 5 = 25
6. 8 x 2 = 16

Brodie's Fast Five

1. 25
2. 45
3. 15
4. 55
5. 60

Page 38 • Progress Test 6

1. 1 x 2 = 2
   2 x 2 = 4
   3 x 2 = 6
   4 x 2 = 8
   5 x 2 = 10
   6 x 2 = 12
   7 x 2 = 14
   8 x 2 = 16
   9 x 2 = 18
   10 x 2 = 20
   11 x 2 = 22
   12 x 2 = 24

2. 1 x 5 = 5
   2 x 5 = 10
   3 x 5 = 15
   4 x 5 = 20
   5 x 5 = 25
   6 x 5 = 30
   7 x 5 = 35
   8 x 5 = 40
   9 x 5 = 45
   10 x 5 = 50
   11 x 5 = 55
   12 x 5 = 60

Page 39 • Multiplying and dividing: the two times table

1. 2
2. 4
3. 6
4. 8
5. 10
6. 12
7. 14
8. 16
9. 18
10. 20
11. 22
12. 24
13. 2
14. 3
15. 4
16. 5
17. 6
18. 7
19. 8
20. 9
21. 10
22. 11
23. 12

Page 40 • Multiplying and dividing: the five times table

1. 5
2. 10
3. 15
4. 20
5. 25
6. 30
7. 35
8. 40
9. 45
10. 50
11. 55
12. 60
13. 2
14. 3
15. 4
16. 5
17. 6
18. 7
19. 8
20. 9
21. 10
22. 11
23. 12

Page 41 • Multiplying and dividing: the ten times table

1. 10
2. 20
3. 30
4. 40
5. 50
6. 60
7. 70
8. 80
9. 90
10. 100
11. 110
12. 120
13. 2
14. 3
15. 4
16. 5
17. 6
18. 7
19. 8
20. 9
21. 10
22. 11
23. 12

Page 42 • Money division with 2p coins

1. 6
2. 2
3. 5
4. 9
5. 4
6. 7
7. 11
8. 3
9. 8
10. 10
11. 12

Brodie's Fast Five

1. 30
2. 80
3. 120
4. 60
5. 100

Page 43 • Money division with 5p coins

1. 12
2. 4
3. 9
4. 2
5. 10
6. 6
7. 3
8. 8
9. 11
10. 7
11. 5

Brodie's Fast Five

1. 6
2. 16
3. 24
4. 12
5. 20

Page 46 • Progress Test 7

1.
1 x 2 = 2
2 x 2 = 4
3 x 2 = 6
4 x 2 = 8
5 x 2 = 10
6 x 2 = 12
7 x 2 = 14
8 x 2 = 16
9 x 2 = 18
10 x 2 = 20
11 x 2 = 22
12 x 2 = 24

1 x 5 = 5
2 x 5 = 10
3 x 5 = 15
4 x 5 = 20
5 x 5 = 25
6 x 5 = 30
7 x 5 = 35
8 x 5 = 40
9 x 5 = 45
10 x 5 = 50
11 x 5 = 55
12 x 5 = 60

1 x 10 = 10
2 x 10 = 20
3 x 10 = 30
4 x 10 = 40
5 x 10 = 50
6 x 10 = 60
7 x 10 = 70
8 x 10 = 80
9 x 10 = 90
10 x 10 = 100
11 x 10 = 110
12 x 10 = 120

2. 9
3. 3
4. 7
5. 8
6. 3
7. 11